THE LA

a poem

Abigail A. Zammit

STACK
BOOKS

To my mother and father
and to all Guatemalans of the
past, present and future.

Published 2007
by

Smokestack Books
PO Box 408, Middlesbrough TS5 6WA
e-mail : info@smokestack-books.co.uk
www.smokestack-books.co.uk

Cover design by James Cianciaruso

Printed by
EPW Print & Design Ltd

ISBN 0-9551061-8-4
ISBN 978-0-955-10618-7

Smokestack Books
gratefully acknowledges the support of
Middlesbrough Borough Council
and Arts Council North East

Smokestack Books is a member of
Independent Northern Publishers
www.northernpublishers.co.uk
and is represented by Inpress Ltd
www.inpressbooks.co.uk

'Memories, like corpses, can be exhumed. If they come fragmented or incomplete, it is part of their story.'

(Daniel Wilkinson, *Silence on the Mountain*)

'But how can I tell their story
if I was not there?...
I was looking at them from another country
and I cannot tell their story...
Show me a word I can use.
Show me one verb...
Let them speak for themselves.'

(Ariel Dorfman, 'Vocabulary')

Prologue

Assassination is an extreme measure not normally used in clandestine operations. It should be assumed that it will never be ordered or authorized by any U.S. Headquarters, though the latter may in rare instances agree to its execution by members of an associated foreign service. This reticence is partly due to the necessity for committing communications to paper. No assassination instructions should ever be written or recorded. (CIA and Assassinations: The Guatemalan 1954 Documents, released in 1997)

Between January and November 1980 alone some 3000 people described by government representatives as 'subversives' and 'criminals' were either shot on the spot in political assassinations or seized and murdered later. ('Guatemala: A Government Program of Political Murder', Amnesty International, 1981)

It is possible to kill a man with the bare hands... However, the simplest local tools are often much the most efficient means of assassination. A hammer, axe, wrench, screw driver, fire poker, kitchen knife, lamp stand, or anything hard, heavy and handy will suffice. A length of rope or wire or a belt will do if the assassin is strong and agile. All such improvised weapons have the important advantage of availability and apparent innocence. (CIA and Assassinations)

'They dragged them out and knifed them. They stabbed and cut them as if they were animals and they were laughing as they killed them. They killed them with a machete that had no teeth. They put one old man on a table, and cut open his chest, the poor man, and he was still alive, and so they started to cut his throat... slowly. He was suffering a lot. They were cutting people under the ribs, and blood came rushing out and they were laughing... How the blood ran! It ran all over me'. (Testimony received by Amnesty International concerning the Guatemalan army's massacre of 350 people in July 1982)

Murder is not morally justifiable. Self-defence may be argued if the victim has knowledge which may destroy the resistance organization if divulged. Assassination of persons responsible for atrocities or reprisals may be regarded as just punishment. Killing a political leader whose burgeoning career is a clear and present danger to the cause of freedom may be held necessary. (CIA and Assassinations)

'Do you think we've left proof? In Argentina, there are witnesses, there are books, there are films, there is proof. Here in Guatemala, there is none of that. There are no survivors.' (Colonel Edgar D'Jalma Dominguez, Head of Office for Army Public Relations)

Part I: Fractured Smiles

'I say, whatever the season
the flowers in my country
are like hunger:
they endure all year.'

(Otto René Castillo)

Portrait of a Child

She stands behind the washing line,
the child who can't smile.

She moves barefoot,
her toes
licking earth.

She's gulped dullness
out of damp air,
the stink of it,
nits in her hair,
the turn of her eyes.

She is bruised skin,
dank fever,
fractured smile.

She's worn her T-shirt for three years,
she is tattered cotton cloth.

She hides,
she grabs,
she leaves.

She is seven chicks pecking in a yard,
ten piglets on a rich man's farm.

She is the child who's lost her smile.

The Missionaries I

We no longer turn a blind eye.
We have multifold vision.
We are pilgrims.
We rejoice in knowing.

We look.
And behold.

'Smile for the pictures.
Wait for another.
Una foto, por favor.
Estamos en San Jerónimo,
Estamos en Guatemala.

This is a poor family.
The woman at the door
is the girl's mother.
She smiles for us.'

Her daughter -
the girl that won't smile.

Somos misioneros.
Tenemos Jesus.

The Mother Speaks

Rich strangers come our way,
their colours at our doorstep.

I stand up,
hold my youngest
to my sagging breasts,
I lock my hands,
cover my nipples,
I smile, slightly,
that they might not see
my rotten teeth,
my swollen gums,
my faded dress,
my dirt,
my shame.

They come without warning.

I was once beautiful.
My red dress had black flowers,
he had a white shirt -
we made love.

I was once happy.

The sun stroked my belly -
my baby had blue eyes,
her breath like milk.
Now they are brown -
she has stopped speaking

I am ugly.
My eyes are broken.
No tengo ojos.
No quiero ver.

We were once happy.

My daughter, my daughter.

A Young Missionary

I am a foreigner in the land of trees -
a green stranger.
I hand drinks in plastic bottles,
food for a week or two,
love that might not touch them.

They reach out for more,
sometimes -
they cry out for more,
hands tapping at my shoulders,
sampling my hair -
but not always.
They are shy,
they do not grab.
They smile,
knowingly.

This is their forest -
their luscious greenery,
their stagnant water.

I can carry a brick,
mix mud and mortar,
teach an English word,
play the missionary.
So many people.
One priest
to clothe them.

Not one God.
Not one God.

Hymn

Sheets drape the ceiling,
voices strum the air,
que alegría eres tú, Señor -
the Lord is our joy,
this church bears no cross.

El padre, yesterday, small and frail,
lifted a wafer outside a hut;
we walked inside, tripping on sheets,
mud floor holding table and two chairs,
sunlight streaming square window,
red lipstick on a wooden shelf.

Girls come along in party dresses,
hair black and shining,
plaited, flowing down their backs.
Mothers carry toddlers
in white, pink frills,
ribbons on each pigtail,
mismatched socks, grimy.
Men always outnumbered,
lingering in the shade.
Que alegría eres tú, Señor -
young men eye girls,
us and them singing.

Today, *el padre*, dark and frail,
takes Christ to a stone church.
Sheets drape the ceiling,
voices strum the air,
white hands reach out
for brown ones -
la paz, la paz.

Six rows of children,
a dog by the door.
I smell ripe papayas
and stagnant water;
no party dresses
or plastic flowers.
Que alegría eres tú, Señor -
after mass we throw a party.
They sit outside and wait;
I do not know what food they seek -
wine and orange taste the same.

She comes, too,
the mother of the girl who will not smile,
and the girl with no smile -
her hands reach out,
she eats without talking,
her eyes are ancient,
the dog behind her,
silent,
waiting its turn.
Food for a week or two.

I carry biscuits, bread, biros.
I carry boxes and a fractured smile.

Que alegría eres tú, Señor -
the Lord is our joy,
this church bears no cross.

Padre Alfonso

Death, here, is not the same -
not as we know it.
When time calls, you make it simpler -
you hold a man's hand and let him pass
into the next world.
They thank you for the blankets,
the prayers, the sip of water,
and when they smile
you know you've done nothing.
God laid His hand upon this man
and he stepped away
with his dead cattle and his flea-dog.

The Missionaries II

We sleep on mattresses
sprawled in classrooms,
wake to the crowing
of a hundred cocks,
the incessant barking of dogs,
shower in makeshift bathrooms,
huge frogs croaking on seats at night-time,
us queuing outside at five
waiting for water to trickle down
our backs - fickle but warm -
like tropical rain, smelling of trees
and purple sunsets.

Noon: roads lie roasting in the heat,
sun milks sweat off aching backs,
twenty metres from the school house.
Cement grows clammy, thick,
settles firmly on bricks as we
lay them down, course work precise,
symmetrical, except in gaps
where quadruple rods stick out, vertical -
they will bend and rock, not break -
earthquakes here are easy as disease.

Students, upstairs, prick brown fingers,
teachers struggle with their español -
you can sew your own dress
if you have the fabric,
you can build your own house
if you have wood and tools,
you can type letters once you get a job -
and the politicians sing, recruiting truckloads
of children, bribing them with sweets,
booming music from Europe's Top Twenty,

they'll track down drainage, fix the roads,
while sixteen typists in the classroom
write letters of apology, of complaint,
requests they will, or will not make,
tapping the keys like rain, velvet rain
stroking the grass, cleaning leaves.

And the dogs will bark,
and the cocks will crow.
This is the land of plenty.

Juana

My husband said
we'd have one child -
Nadie, for hope,
for the smell of fresh linen,
the crack of white sheets.
that warm night in January
when his fingers
lingered on my throat
after the priest
blessed the wedding rings.

It was the day
they'd signed
the Peace Accords;
Padre Alfonso
laid his hands
upon our fingers
saying hope
was corn seeds
in our souls,
change - the years
it takes to reap it.

So there was change, peace,
there was freedom;
there were corn seeds
in my husband's fields,
warmth in my house.
There were *frijoles* -
but not for all of us.
I watched my neighbours
crying, starving, dying,
thought of Padre's words,
screamed at night-time,

dreamt I lived in straw huts
gave birth to dying infants.

When they brought me
Nadie, wailing,
her red face puckered,
wrinkled,
I thought of change,
I stretched
my arms for her.
Nadie - for hope,
for the smell of fresh linen,
the crack of white sheets
the night we made love
after the priest
blessed the wedding rings.

She is strong,
this child of ours -
her father has plans for her.
She knows our neighbours,
plays with their children,
asks me why they drink water
out of stagnant pools,
sit in the streets,
while she has a home,
food, a clarinet.
I tell her, 'I have
no answers, child,
your father helps,
we donate money
we aid the missionaries.
Be kind to them.
I have no answers'.

Her father says
she'll soon be old enough
to see the world,
travel to Europe,
understand how people live
elsewhere.
I fear she might get lost,
feel homesick,
crave papayas
and maize tortillas.
Still, I'll let her go,
I want her to know,
to understand.
We do this for her.
We have no answers.

Part II: Breaking the Silence

'I was a tear of my country
Rolling down the face of America.'

(Otto René Castillo)

Workers on a Coffee Plantation

Saber. Saber.
Who knows?
We know nothing.
There has been no war.
Not on this plantation.
Not in this area.
There are no guerrillas.
Only the army.

Saber. Saber.
No. We haven't heard the bullets,
and if you've heard them
let me tell you,
this is God's will;
everywhere, people fight -
there's war too,
somewhere in Eastern Europe.
Let's pray.
Let's read the Bible:
'There shall be wars
and rumours of wars.'
It explains it here.

Saber. Saber.
No casualties in La Patria.
There's been no fighting.
No machetes, no bullets.
These are coffee plantations.
We have berries, shade trees.
The landowners are good to us.
They keep us safe.
We live in peace.
We belong to them.
There's been no shooting.

Saber. Saber.
Who knows?
Ask elsewhere

American Journalist, 1994

This was Cabrera's coffee nation
of enforced debts, drafted workers.
When the coffee prices fell,
officials paid you a visit,
forced you to the plantations.

These are *La Patria, El Progreso, La Igualdad* -
Nation, Progress, Equality -
coffee plantations where people toil
but have no salaries.

The *patrones* are German, the workers
Indians turned Ladinos, *naturales* -
dispossessed, wrenched from the Highlands,
from the spirits of their ancestors.

Yesterday, *La Patria* was a battlefield,
bullets were flying in *El Progreso*,
people killed each other in *La Igualdad*.
'What about the war,' I ask, 'the army,
the guerrillas, yesterday's fighting?'

'*Saber*,' they tell me. Not in this area.
Not on this plantation. *Saber. Saber.*
There is denial, the untelling of stories.
Where terror reigns, there is forgetting.

Sister Isabel

You must watch their eyes -
not their nods of approval,
their silence when questioned,
the rigid smiles,
the tensing of muscles -
but the eyes that swell and shine
like the glossy eyeballs
of religious statues
in an empty chapel.

Spokesperson for Amnesty International I

Listen to the swish of skirts in the breeze,
mark the headscarves perked against the sun,
the green intensity of coffee leaves as they grow bigger
and wider like the fast forward in a nature documentary,
white flowers dropping to turn into berries,
the feel of sweaty hands pulling ripe fruit,
our silent reapers framed and reframed
until they are no longer solitary and confined
but the witnesses of an exploited population,
the toil of ten hours of temporary work a day,
the shroud of hunger swelling towards the huts.

José

Mire, usted, I'll tell you the truth, answer your questions;
when you're old and dying, there's nothing to fear.
During the revolution, I worked in *La Patria*;
we held meetings, appointed leaders, learnt the right
to demand change, to expect salaries. 'The lands
to those who work them!' '*Que Vive el campañero Arbenz*,
soldier of the people!' When the patrón didn't pay,
we went on strike; we would not grovel at his feet,
we would not let him hit us, treat us like pigs -
this was our land, we had a right to it. There was
change and hope and daring, till Arbenz fell, landowners
kicked the rebels out. For months I couldn't feed my family.

After that, there was war, slow at first, hesitant,
then there were killings, fraudulent elections, people
disappearing. The youngsters grew angry, took to arms,
hid in the mountains; at first they'd kill a cow,
distribute the meat, paint stray dogs as slogans.
Sometimes they killed landowners, the cruel ones.
In the end, they grew wiser, trained like the militia,
fought and died like men who had nothing to lose.
For they had nothing. Their people had nothing.
Expropriated land returned to the *patrones'* hands.
We had nothing. *Mire, usted*, this is the truth.
When you're old and dying, there's nothing to fear.

Kaibil Soldier

If I advance, follow me.
If I hesitate, push me forward.
If I retreat, kill me.

It was our anthem -
we took pride in it,
sang it out loud.
When lips went dry
and fear parched throats,
we worded it silently,
advancing slowly,
surrounding the enemy.

Most often, though,
we didn't see them.
We were out for days,
being shot at, ambushed,
running into mines.

I got scared,
not seeing them -
blindness is fear.
And there they were
all the time, hiding,
trying to get me.

If I advance, follow me.
If I hesitate, push me forward.
If I retreat, kill me.

We were the elite,
owned helicopters,
launched rockets,
threw grenades.

The guerrillas
knew the mountains,
mimicked birdcalls,
read footprints,
scampered like rabbits.

All we saw were the people,
villagers who let them hide,
who'd not betray them.
So the people were the enemy.
In Sacuchum we killed the enemy.
We followed orders.
We had no choice.

If I advance, follow me.
If I hesitate, push me forward.
If I retreat, kill me.

In Sacuchum I killed the enemy.

Survivors

Because this is Sacuchum
- Sacuchum de los Dolores -
we speak the past, listen.
Sacuchum of the Sorrows,
write down our pain.
We speak and fear, but we speak,
because no-one ever heard us,
because we didn't hear the gunshots.

On New Year's Day
there were battles in the woods.
We listened to the army
bombing the mountainside.
The next day, soldiers
walked up the hills,
surrounded the valley.
By Sunday morning
they burst into town,
pulled us by the hair,
dragged us out of our houses,
grabbed radios, clothes, money,
whatever they found.

They pointed guns at us,
so we followed them
to the church square.
The captain at the belfry shouted:
'The guerrillas have been here!
We know this for certain!
We know too, fish only live
where there is water.
You are the water.
We'll dry the pond
to kill the fish.
We'll take care of you.'

They herded us
to the soccer field,
where we stood
before officials,
civilians with hoods.
Soldiers called out names:
'Is this the one?'
and they grabbed people.
The rest of us
sent to our homes,
ordered not to leave.
No lights, no fires.
We couldn't cook.
We couldn't sleep.
We spent the night
worrying, waiting.
The next morning
we were out, searching.

Because this is Sacuchum
- Sacuchum de los Dolores -
we speak the past, listen.
Sacuchum of the Sorrows,
write down our pain.
We speak and fear, but we speak,
because no-one ever heard us,
because we didn't hear the gunshots.

He was my father,
my brother, my son,
my husband -
his throat slit,
his tongue cut out,
five bodies to a ditch.
She was my girlfriend,
my daughter, my sister -
tied to a tree,

raped and beaten,
strangled with cords.
Six to a ditch.

We speak and fear, but we speak,
because this was Sacuchum -
Sacuchum de los Dolores.
Because no-one knows the facts,
because lies should be untold,
because history should be written.
We are Sacuchum still,
still we are Sacuchum -
Sacuchum de los Dolores.

Guerrillero

Every day I died a little,
I was consumed.
I asked the patron
for a minimum wage -
he paid for my football gear.

So we wrote ORPA on the walls.
Every day we died a little bit,
we were consumed.
The volcano was our seal;
we were the eruption,
fighting injustice,
the enemies of the people,
the government, the army,
the rich, the foreign power.

Workers received us warmly:
'Qué viva ORPA!'
We wanted revolution,
a better education,
better health, better salaries,
the right to work our land.
So we wrote ORPA on the walls.
We were the eruption.

Our fathers were gentleman -
they fought with words.
'Viva la paz!' they said,
and disappeared.
So we wrote ORPA on the walls.
'Everyone to war now!'
We had no choice.
We were the eruption.

We fought the army,
hiding in the woods,
training in secret.
The people didn't speak -
in Sacuchum we hid for months,
walked the woods with the *cusheros*.
They guarded our secret.

In Sacuchum they killed our people.
So we wrote ORPA on the walls.
Every day we died a little bit,
we were consumed.
The volcano was our seal.
We were the eruption.

General Gramajo

Listen sonny, this is not the States -
some things that seem abnormal in one place,
are quite normal in another.
In the eighties, we suppressed guerrillas,
traced their communist supporters;
that might have included disappearing people,
torturing some to get to the spider.
Every country does it,
so don't come preaching to me
about peace and human rights.
I've been to Harvard,
I know about your war tactics.
Wasn't it you helped us
sweep away the communist regime,
CIA agents training the army?

One has to be changeable,
like a serpent shedding skin.
Take me, for instance,
I was a soldier and a general,
studying in your country
on five separate occasions;
I was elected minister of defence,
advocate of mild measures,
champion of democratic thinking.
Have you ever heard of
'The Dance of the Conquest',
the Spanish defeating the Mayas?
As a child, I loved watching it,
always wanted to play the part
of the *Ajis*, funny red monkey -
not Spanish, not indigenous -
the one that pesters everyone.

Listen sonny, flexibility is the key -
those that preach violence
when it's past its time
are a threat to the state.
I've told our elite businessmen
the military is no longer their concubine.
We are professional soldiers -
it wasn't easy for us either,
making concessions
when we had won the war,
but as I tell you, one has to move on,
our image abroad is what we cherish,
especially now when that conniving
Menchú woman has turned the world
against us, telling her lies to a biographer,
getting herself the Nobel for peace.
Puuuu! That we've come to this!

You will see, sonny, all too soon,
friends will turn their back on you
covering their dirty ass when they can
no longer squeeze your juice out!
Take me, for instance - they had the face
to summon me to court demanding
forty-seven million dollars in damages.
Puta! If I paid that sum of money,
how much would McNamara have to pay
for what his troops did in Vietnam?
Me in my country, him in another!
How much would Cheney have to pay
for what his troops did in Panama?
This is not a question of law -
it's a question of power.

Look at my *Thesis of National Stability*;
I know this country's history
like the insides of my pockets.
Gringos come, pointing a finger.
Puta! Fix Guatemala's
five-hundred years of problems if you can!
Listen sonny, all the army did
was defend the army -
an *Ajis* saving its skin.
We even held general elections,
allowed the Christian Democrats to win.
Puta, I say! The army is the victim!

An Indian Soldier

I brought them a pink panty,
the lace stained a dirty yellow.
One officer guffawed,
ruffled my hair,
'Now you are a man,
a true soldier,' he said, 'make sure
you rub that little cock of yours
with lemon, keeps the venom
of your Indian hussies out.'

After that, they stopped
spitting in my food,
mixing chilli with my *tortillas*,
ramming my elbow
into my stomach; instead,
I handled new recruits - boys my age -
tied their feet with sticks as I
pushed them to their knees,
placed snakes around their necks,
lowered rubber hoods
onto their heads.

You cannot be a soldier
if you're not strong enough
to withstand interrogation.
You might cry, shout
for your mother, beg for mercy,
but mutter an officer's name
under fear of torture,
and you're as good as dead.

The first time I killed a man,
I screamed like a woman.
The colonel laughed, said I'd

cure myself through practice.
I left the *cuartel* feeling very macho,
insulted people, took no shit
from civilians. They made me
a Corporal; I delivered messages
for the kidnapping of people.

When I returned to my village,
I could no longer hang out with guys
who weren't in the army:
we saw things differently. Some said
we should have stayed at home,
become civil patrollers.
I thought, better be a recruit
with sixty *quetzales* in your pocket,
than a civil patroller,
unpaid, unarmed,
with everything to lose.

American Journalist before
the Truth Commission

The night before, we paid the *espiritista* a visit;
she explained the difference between good and evil magic,
her table laid out in black, drowning in candles,
a dozen portraits of the Virgin Mary, crosses,
saints sitting with Maximón.

'No, gracias,' I told her, 'I'd rather you didn't
let the spirits speak'; I thought of the departed,
how if this wasn't superstition, they'd recount
the various ways in which they had been killed.
I'd document the evidence.

That night I couldn't sleep, recalled the morning's threats,
the voice on the phone, bottle shards at the door,
a widow approaching me at the market, asking me
whether the meeting was safe; my answer, quick,
'Yes. Nothing to fear.'

I checked the room for cockroaches, everywhere
except the ceiling. Something fell on my neck,
scurried up my face, I jumped out, smashed it
with my boot. Thought of carcasses in mass graves.
Relatives too scared to speak.

I slept, dreamt I was driving, the car cracking open,
crumbling, the bed moving, the whole room,
back and forth. I rushed. It was the *brujo's* curse.
The spirits of the dead. Mourners pointing fingers.
The death squad was after me.

Voices from the Truth Commission

The day Montt and Ronald Reagan met,
Kaibil soldiers marched to Las Dos Erres.
Forsenics, years later, exhumed 162 people.

'People lived in constant fear -
after eight, nobody ventured out,
not even to the latrines.'

'My husband fought for the workers -
soldiers marched to our house, took off
the roof while I was going into labour.'

'They made my neighbours kneel at wells,
smashed their heads with sledge hammers,
send them plunging inside to join the pile.'

'I was just eight; they put a hood over my head -
at first I wouldn't point them out,
but the officer threatened - I was scared.'

'Soldiers beat the stomachs of pregnant women,
kept the girls and women captive,
raped them repeatedly for three days.'

'It was my whole body - I'd get cold,
sweat for no reason. My sister woke me up
gently, tapping a stick against the wall.'

'I pace the room, I do not sleep,
I have shrapnel in my chest,
knots in my throat.'

'Hours later, blood on the walls,
placenta and umbilical cords,
moribund cries from stagnant wells.'

'What about the army massacres?'
they asked Chapin - 'Those incidents
simply haven't taken place.'

Testimonio

'My name is Rigoberta Menchú. I am twenty-three years old. This is my testimony. I didn't learn it from a book and I didn't learn it alone.'

(Rigoberta Menchú)

My ears the pinholes of hearing loss,
my memory the battered brain of the repressed,
my eyes the suppressed tears of a blindfolded son,
my mouth the sour bile of men on the death list.

My fingers shape and retell,
mould the past, set it within reason.
For if I tell the truth, what will you say?
This plot too scanty for so many deaths,
too senseless for fiction.

I reinvent myself in search of truths - justice for the dead.
I have my heroes, my villains, victims and oppressors.
But we are one - indeed we are one.
It is not who killed and why, it is the dead -
the wooden crosses lining church walls.

And so I speak, I look for answers,
but there is nothing, except the ticking of a clock,
the clipping of nails, the Babylon of distant voices.

A Refugee

We fled from the mountains,
turned our backs to smoke rising
from burnt *milpas*, left the hot earth
where our homes had lain.
The dogs followed, their tails
between their legs, never barking.
At night we slept in the forest,
huddled for warmth, trembled at
every sound. Sebastián and Raúl
carried sticks - they were
the only men left. The third day,
we heard rustling in the woods, the dogs
pricked their ears. Camouflaged soldiers
surrounded us. We could not fight.

Here, we work in the fields,
queue outside for food and drink.
The Major has explained the benefits
of the 'Food-for-Work Program';
he says it's give and take.
The first phase is Beans and Bullets -
Frijoles y Fusiles, then there's
Techo, Tortilla y Trabajo,
meaning 'Roof, Food, and Work';
finally, there's Peace and Harmony,
for us all, *Paz y Tranquilidad*.

The soldiers' eyes are everywhere;
they patrol our own patrols,
keep a watch for subversives,
throw leaflets out of helicopters.
When they call out to us
with megaphones, it's like whistling
to a dog - we leave whatever

we are doing to assemble
in the plaza. They shout orders,
make us denounce communists,
hand machetes to patrollers.
Women cry, tin roofs glisten in the sun,
smoke rises from burnt *milpas*.
We can hardly see the mountains.

A Daily Schedule for the Refugees

We wake them up at five a.m.,
have civic talk and more talk,
breakfast and ideological talk,
civil defence, recreation, health lecture,
how to use toilets, how to boil water,
food preparation and ideological talk,
lunch and ideological talk,
agriculture, recreation, group dynamics,
recreation, and ideological talk,
patriotic symbols lecture, flag lowering,
dinner, ideological thought,
film or marimba entertainment.
Sometimes we play with them.

Major Veliz

Los indios, son como arcilla -
Indians are easy to ply; it is best
to guide them. You wouldn't believe
how subversives indoctrinate them
in the mountains. They themselves
admit it to us. But what happens?
So much fighting, so much suffering!
The children get sick and die,
and there they are in the mountains,
going hungry, thirsty, abandoned
by the enemy. So we get them down,
teach them how to protect themselves
from communists. Here they have food,
houses, peace, quiet. They are happy.
We call these 'model villages'.

Of course, we don't turn them lose
until we think they have totally changed
their ideology. This might take time.
It's not easy to work with the brainwashed.
The most stubborn, I take them myself.
talk to them, teach them through movies:
how people work in the United States,
free, without pressure, and how they work
in Russia, where you see soldiers in the fields
hitting the people, leaders in their big cars
rationing food. 'Do you want to have to live
like this?' I ask. Then they see we are right:
'No,' they reply. We tell them to become
good people; they are good people, really -
what happened is - they were deceived.

Spokesperson for Amnesty International II

Come to this patch of blackened ground -
this stretch of land where nothing grows.
Listen to the dead that live among the rubbish dumps,
a child sniffing glue by a red tractor,
girls wrapping their black hair among dry sugar canes.
See the clotted blood of tortured hands
peeping out of rainbow mattresses,
twelve women keening like distressed seabirds,
babies wrapped in cloth, hanging from branches,
a skeletal horse tied to a tree stump.

Tzalbal Street Map

'How shall I get to the refugee camp?'
'It's easy: walk straight until you find yourself
in Street of the Fallen.
Turn right into Avenue of Hope,
cross the road and turn ninety degrees to your left -
you'll find National Army Avenue.
Walk half a mile and you'll end up
in Friendship Street.
That's where our model village is.'

Independence Day

Nebaj beauty queens in candy-box gowns
sit in the back of a flatbed truck,
smiling like broken China dolls.
People, outside, lean against their blue-pink walls
waiting for the float to go by:
a gigantic army helmet, twelve-foot wide,
followed by marching schoolchildren,
right palms spread on their hearts
as they sing the national anthem.
Boy soldiers linger by the *Ceiba* tree
where three months earlier they shot subversives.
A priestless church hums to the bones
in the backyard, its crucified Christ
bleeding again as a Roman centurion,
once dressed like Kaibil soldier,
thrusts a lance into His flesh.

More floats and marching soldiers,
followed by civil patrollers forcing their face
into the smile of village idiots,
and down we go all the way to the soccer stadium
where Major Tito Arias delivers a speech
on the pride of the nation,
the rainbow *quetzal* singing in lush forests
the *monja blanca* white as Indian virgins,
the beauty of Guatemala marred only
by communists who need to be taught
the good way, and we all listen - the children,
the widows, the elderly, the broken,
and the mountains, which once trembled, now listen.

Bus Ride

At Tecpán,
we stop talking;
the driver throws glances
at the mirror,
his sweaty fingers
clenching the gearbox.
Two soldiers
walk the length of the aisle,
swinging their rifles,
waiting.

Outside, we line up,
lower our heads.
Children grow silent,
clasp their mothers' hands.
We pray, we breathe,
at the mercy of a hooded man.
The soldiers watch him, wait.
He nods, gestures to the woman
who's packed a hen
inside her straw bag. We hear
its peaceful cackling.
The woman cries,
screams.

We do not speak.
the hen cackles -
louder. Screams.
We close our eyes.
We breathe.
We've been spared.
In the distance,
three gun shots.

Silence. We walk back
to the bus, shaking.
We are leaves,
falling.

The Dead

In Zacualpa, soldiers
turn peasants' fields
into our dumping grounds.

Earth takes us, hacked
and bleeding, our corpses
sweetening the soil.

Next harvest,
the corn plentiful,
the fields golden.

The poor starve,
but do not eat. They say
the land is blighted.

Me llaman Guatemala

I am the military, the purification
of subversive villagers, the erasure
of empty towns from a map,
the nation of secret mass graves,
human dumps, sanitized documents.
I am burnt huts, scorched earth.
I am INCO, EXMIBAL.
I am weapons from Israel, Chile, the U.S.
I am Beans and Guns. I am guerrillas.
I am oil, nickel, coffee, cotton.
I am Coca Cola, United Fruit.

I am the drinking of my own
people's blood. I am torn *huipiles*.
I am repression, displacement.
I am genocide. I am Ixil, Quiché, Mam.
I am Indian, German, Ladino.
I am bitter fruit, scorched earth.
I am torture, terror, tragedy.
I am a slave, a beast of burden.
I am a grave marked XXX.
I am my last order,
my own disappearance.

Indian Civil Patroller

'I am a victorious soldier
Of the Civil Defence
Always side by side like a brother
With the brave army.'

(Civil Patrol Anthem)

What have I done?
The voice of my brother's blood
cries to me from the ground.
I have covered his flesh
with stones of forgetfulness,
weighed down memory
with torrents of water,
washed my hands
with lava;
so tell me now
I have no eyes,
no ears, no mouth.
What have I done?
My son, my God,
my Father!
What have I done?

Part III: Stones of Hope

'We swear that freedom will push its naked flower through the violated sand.'

(Mural in a student café at the University of San Carlos)

Stela One

Every time
a man
kills his brother,
a spring of fresh water
dries up
in the mountains
and the *nahual* -
the animal spirit,
cries and disappears.

They walk
alone,
these thieves,
these plunderers,
these sleepwalking
step-sons of the Maya,
who have forgotten
their history,
their inheritance -
there's no afterlife
for the fallen.

Stela Two

'Among the Maya
to cure a fright
you put a fresh-laid egg
in the armpit
of the frightened person
and in that way
the self-worth and health
that the phantom has stolen
will return to the afflicted.

(Victor Montejo)

It would take
a hundred thousand
fresh-laid eggs
placed gently
in the armpits
of the frightened,
the exiled,
the dispossessed,
to make
the bloody grass
turn green,
buds bear
white lilies,
voices sing.

Guatemalteco

Dicen los guías extranjeros -
they say our ancestors
knew the secrets of the universe,
excelled in geometry, astronomy,
built pyramids out of limestone,
temples, houses, doorsteps,
devised glyphs, complex calendars
wove cloth on backstrap looms,
held seed and solstice festivals,
grew squash, corn, chilli pepper,
wrote their version of creation,
before the coming of Christ,
before Spaniards burnt the *Popul Vuh*,
and we forgot 'bout Heart-of-Sky,
who moulded maize to make us human.

I see Mayas in the city now,
women and children selling wares,
tapestries that lure tourists.
I see white people haggle
over beaded bracelets, hairclips,
rainbow accessories
and I wonder what the teachers mean
when they say the land spat on us,
the gods turned sour, that our ancestors
faded with their palaces and tapestries,
starving or warring under the blink
of storms or earthquakes
leaving in their wake
the green canopies of lush jungle,
the jaguar-roars of howler monkeys.
Dicen los profesores, I am Ladino -
half Spanish, half Mayan,
Dicen los guías extranjeros,
todo es misterio.

Foreign Poet on Tikal

You look solemn now,
secret and solemn like jade long lost,
or like your once lusty kings
slipping silently into their underworld,
letting keen archaeologists bear the weight
of history lost and found.

Trees have taken possession of your wealth,
digging roots deep within your structures;
butterflies hover over your fallen empire,
birds make their nests in the recesses
of your abandoned homes.

You look most solemn now,
secret and solemn like texts long lost,
or your disappearing gods,
walking silently to their sacred mountains.
Roots pierce your soul -
a Mayan queen, found and lost,
you are perfect, utterly perfect, now.

Cientos Estelas

Engraved on broken stelae,
the lunar phases of humanity:
the changing rhythms
of volcanic eruptions,
wars, droughts, decease,
the next eclipse,
the longest nightfall.

A hundred pitted stones
written in a language
the *Ah Be* only can decipher,
measuring by fractured wings
of blue-green hummingbirds
a hundred million Indian dead.

Engraved on scattered stelae,
the quiet intricacies of time:
the hours and days and years
it will take blood to blend
perfectly with soil, skeletons
to be exhumed, corn
to beget husks of gold.

Sueño

'And with her smiling face
the most humble peasant girl
will write the love poems
that didn't leave my throat.'

(Otto René Castillo)

So in Castillo's dream,
she smiles -
the girl who will not smile -
brushes her fingertips
along husks of maize
burns incense for Ixchel,
wears a newly woven *huipil*,
goes to school wearing shoes,
spells her name right,
plays the marimba,
speaks Spanish, *Mam*
has no memory of bloodshed,
mutilated corpses,
civil war,
she smiles -
a gold-rimmed smile.
She isn't orphaned,
isn't silenced.
She's made of corn.
She can't be broken

Epilogue

*'May the people have
Peace and be happy! '*

(The *Popul Vuh*)

Today, the smell of lavender blends with steam from the
shower, positions me under the warm rain, the day I got
soaked running to the school-house, or the queue to the
showers after brick-laying.

I remember the afternoon I lay outside on a mattress,
Nadie's mother coming to speak to me, advising me to take
her medicine, and the night Jean woke me up, pointing to
the phosphorescence quivering in a corner; Amy, next
morning, telling me it was a sign from the dead.

How the night I was ill I dreamt I was counting nits buried
in the hair of the girl who would not smile, how I got it into
my head she was about to die and she smiled in her passing,
sighing briefly, like a newborn.

Now I think of dark-skinned women smiling graciously, the
child in a tattered T-shirt, the girl with the broken smile,
six-year-old Diana kissing me goodbye, and I recall the
purple tinge of lavender, the perfume of that foreign land,
las voces, purple, from the land of trees.

Notes

Several of the poems in Part II are based on events and interviews in Daniel Wilkinson, *Silence on the Mountain: Stories of Terror, Betrayal and Forgetting in Guatemala* (Duke University Press, 2004).

The Mayan legend described in 'Stela One' is mentioned in a poem by Victor Montejo in *Sculpted Stones* (Curbstone Press, 1995).

A 'nahual' or 'tonal' is an animal companion or alter ego given to children when they are born according to the ancient Mayan calendar.

The 'Ah Be' mentioned in 'Cientos Estelas' are Mayan priests or diviners.

Further Reading

Otto René Castillo, *Tomorrow Triumphant: Selected Poems* (Night Horn Books, 1984)

David B Castledine (trans) *Popul Vuh: The Sacred Book of the Ancient Mayas-Quiché* (Monclem Ediciones, 2001)

Nick Cullather, *Secret History: The CIA's Classified Account of its Operations in Guatemala 1952-54* (Stanford University Press, 2006)

Susanne Jonas, Ed McCaughan and Elizabeth Sutherland Martinez (eds) *Guatemala: Tyranny on Trial - Testimony of the Permanent People's Tribunal* (Synthesis Publications, 1984)

Michael Silverstone, *Rigoberta Menchú: Defending Human Rights in Guatemala* (Feminist Press, 1999)

Jean-Marie Simon, *Guatemala: Eternal Spring, Eternal Tyranny* (Norton, 1987)

Daniel Wilkinson, *Silence on the Mountain: Stories of Terror, Betrayal and Forgetting in Guatemala* (Duke University Press, 2004)